MW01487715

The Indie Esoteric

A Guide to Self Publishing for Aspiring Occult Authors

S. Connolly

The Indie Esoteric

A Guide to Self Publishing for Aspiring Occult Authors

S. Connolly

Ψ

DB PUBLISHING 2017

MMXVII

DB Publishing is an arm of Darkerwood Publishing Group, PO Box 2011, Arvada, CO 80001.

ISBN: 978-1545570234

Book Design by Stephanie Reisner

About this Book

I am often approached for advice on self-publishing, especially by aspiring occult authors. Because I really dislike having the same conversations repeatedly, I decided to write down the answers to the most common questions I'm asked. It started as a collection of blog posts (no longer available), and I finally decided to turn it into a book at the request of several people.

This book is a collection of those blog posts (no longer available) that I wrote on independent self-publishing of esoteric books. It also includes advice for aspiring authors, a discussion about eBook theft and how it adversely affects authors, and my own views of the esoteric publishing climate in 2017.

Hopefully it will help new and aspiring occult authors take those first steps toward publication.

Introduction

Yesterday I had a conversation with a writer friend who also pens esoteric material. We were discussing the nature of "occult" small presses. The problem, it seems, is that a lot of esoteric authors write really niche stuff. Some of it so controversial, that the more mainstream professional esoteric publishers won't touch that material with a ten-foot pole.

This puts many esoteric authors in a prime position to be preyed upon by start-up small presses and small presses that are everything but professional in their conduct. Some of these small presses don't even bother with editing or layout (insisting authors do their own) and they don't provide marketing support leaving authors wondering why they're even bothering with a small press anyway, other than to give a cut of their profits (oftentimes half or more) to someone who did very little work on the project.

My philosophy is this – if you're going to do it all yourself anyway – why should you bother involving a publisher? With a little extra effort, you can take your work into your own hands and likely sell just as many copies if you do it right.

Let's face it – you already have the audience. If you didn't, a lot of these small presses wouldn't even bother with you. They tend to go after bigger names; people who have written books who have a reputation in the community. On that note: If you don't have an audience, you will have to build it from scratch and that comes from frequenting forums, talking to people, and having a strong web-presence.

So, in this book, *The Indie Esoteric*, I'm going to explain the process to you, step-by-step, so you can take charge of your books and their publication and keep the control where it belongs – with you. Long gone are the days where you had to suck it up when your publisher hadn't paid you in months, you hadn't seen a sales report in forever, or when your book came out a year after its scheduled release date. No more.

Of course, you are going to have to do more work, and at first there is a learning curve. But I'm confident that if you are at least mildly tech-savvy, you can put out the SAME quality (if not better) books by yourself as you would get going through a small press. The best part is you don't have to involve a middle man and you don't even have to have thousands in startup funds, or room in your garage to store hundreds of books, to be successful or get distribution.

First, let's acknowledge that those who are reading this are likely practitioners, priests, and magicians first, writers second, publishers last. I also realize that no one goes into writing esoteric texts with the idea that they're going to make crap-loads of money (unless they're rather delusional). However, it's perfectly realistic for esoteric authors to expect to be paid for their work, because they're producing teaching material for occult students. It's time esoteric authors stop apologizing for this and embrace that they do deserve to be compensated for their many hours of research, writing time, experience, and the hours spent in the temple getting their hands dirty. The only people who would argue otherwise haven't created anything, therefore their opinions don't matter.

That said, let's begin. I'm going to break book into several sections as follows:

- Introduction – How to get started. (This is what you're reading now.)
- Printers & Distributors – We're going to talk about six or seven websites every esoteric Indie author should know about, and how each one can benefit you. Then we'll talk about limited edition hardcovers.
- Editing & Formatting – Creating eBooks and interior files to please your printers and your readers. I'll also share some of my quick and dirty tips to save you time and make your process more efficient.
- Cover Art – Some hints and suggestions for nice covers that look pro.

- Launching & Marketing – How to launch and market your books to reach the largest possible audience.

Let's talk about getting started.

There are two definite things you need before you begin your journey into the world of Indie Esoteric publishing.
1. A completed, fully edited manuscript and
2. Some dedicated time to learn the process.

You don't necessarily need a block of ISBNs or thousands of dollars in start-up money. The big secret is you can put out paperbacks, eBooks, and hardcovers at virtually no cost to you IF you know what you're doing.

So first let's talk about your goals in publishing your book.

Do you want to reach the largest possible audience? If so, consider making your book available to readers in multiple formats and through multiple distributors. I will talk more about this later, but ultimately, I want to point out that not all readers can afford limited edition hardcovers, and while the royalty on LEH (Limited Edition Hardcovers) are higher, you have to do twice as much work and you will earn every penny you make. Not only that but it could take you anywhere from 1-5 years to sell that entire stock to make the money you think you might make. So, do consider that if you think there's a get-rich-quick scheme there.

Do you want to print a fine bound edition?
If so you'll obviously do short print runs as opposed to print-on-demand, and you'll leave eBooks and paperbacks out of the equation unless you plan on including something in the fine bound edition that the paperbacks and/or eBooks won't have. I'll discuss short print runs more in the following pages. If you do want fine bound editions, expect that you will need between $2,500-$5,000 in startup funds depending on the cost of the print run.

Do you want to print a book for a specific group of people and not the general public?
Lulu.com (who we'll talk about more in this book) has an option you can set at the very beginning of the process where the only people who can purchase a book must have the URL to do so. There's also an option for you to keep the book to yourself. That might be handy if you want to print special hardcovers for friends or family, or make your own limited editions on demand. Mind you the quality equates to cheaper cloth covered hardcover and nothing fancy.

Do you want your own publishing imprint?
One that you'll use just to print your own books under? People do this for a lot of reasons. One reason is to hide the fact that they're self-published, because they read everywhere that there's no respect in self-publishing. You know who keeps perpetuating this myth that only traditionally published authors are

worth anything? Traditional publishers and those who make their money working with traditional publishers. Readers rarely give two craps about who your publisher is (especially when it comes to non-fiction) if the books are good and give them the information they want. So, if you want to start your own imprint it is as simple as filling out some forms and buying a block of ISBNs from bowker.com. No, you don't have to start an official company to do this. You are you, dba (doing business as) your imprint. For those of you who didn't know before – now you know how simple it is to become a publisher. Which explains why there are so many bad ones out there. Literally ANYONE and their mother can become a "publisher". Even people who don't like to read and have no business experience whatsoever.

Do you want to make sure everything you publish is protected by official copyright? This is pretty simple, too. Just go on over to the copyright office website at www.copyright.gov, fill out a form, and once you've published your book, you take a couple of copies of the published book, send it to them with a filled-out form and a filing fee (follow the instructions) and they send you back an official certificate telling the world that your book is yours. Of course, technically your work is covered the moment you have it written. Some people will tell you to mail yourself a copy of your MS and then never open it and the postmark will be your proof of copyright. You can do that, too.

Now here are some things you should expect when self-publishing.

1. **It's a lot of work.** Now you're not just writing it, you are doing all of it from the initial idea to the final product. As you learn, you'll begin to streamline your process. So, while you may spend days putting out your first self-published book, this does not include the time it takes to write the book obviously, the fourth one may only take you a few hours.

2. **There will be unexpected snags and delays.** Sometimes printers run behind schedule. You may accidentally upload a manuscript to Kindle that has a glaring typo. Shit happens and it will continue to happen. Just remember that most everything can be fixed, and those errors that can't easily be fixed (like a typo in a short print run that you discover after it's been printed) make each project its own unique animal. Learn to be adaptable and forgive yourself. Those who adapt survive in this business. Those who don't will drown.

3. **There will always be that one asshole** who throws it in your face that you use Lulu and/or Createspace or even Ingram. People who do that are arrogant, snotty pieces of crap, and should be ignored (and laughed at).

However – I guarantee that self-publishing is a rewarding experience and if you're a control freak, like me, you'll prefer it to dealing with small presses. Your pocketbook may thank you too as you may suddenly find you're able to make at least a partial living (or even a grocery trip) from all your hard work. You'll also have access to real time sales and you'll be able to plan your budget since most distribution services pay monthly if you've met their threshold (i.e. minimum amount before they pay).

Now that we've discussed some basics, it's time for you to sign up for your "publishing" accounts with all the printing and distribution outlets.

Printers and Distributors

Next, we're going to talk about your first steps into independently publishing your latest esoteric book. So, you have a finished manuscript and you have some time. Now mind you you're NOT going to upload your manuscript today. No, today you're simply going to decide what type of printing and distribution services you need and sign up accordingly. Your manuscript still needs a good edit, polish and formatting before we can upload that sucker anyway. One step at a time.

Let me introduce you to some publishing terms. By printing service, I mean a service that prints your book regardless the type of printing technology they use. When I'm talking offset print runs (or short print runs) I am talking about books that are printed by a service and sent to you, and you do your own distribution. When I talk about POD (Print on Demand) I'm talking about a service that distributes your books for you and prints each book as it is ordered by your customer. Print-on-demand technology is a much more efficient and earth-friendly way to print books. That way you don't lose valuable space in your house storing the books, you don't lose time having to play distributor, and you aren't left with anything you can't sell. For most projects, print-on-demand printing/distribution services are the way to go. The only exception to that is if you want to do your own distribution 100%, or you want to put out a Limited-Edition Hardcover. Offset print runs/short print runs require you to put out money up front, which you then make back by selling the books (out of your garage, trunk, or online store) at markup. Print-on-demand services don't really charge authors anything, unless you want copies for yourself, or in the case of Lulu, they ask you to buy a physical "proof" of the book if you want their free distribution service.

A "proof" is a sample book printed using the files you provided to show you how each book looks when printed. You will be asked to "proof" each book before it goes to print, but many of these places have online pdf proofs that you can look at before it goes to print.

Finally, a distributor is a company that takes and fulfills orders on your behalf. In the case of the following websites – your printer/distributor will often be the same company. They will provide you with monthly sales reports and monthly (or quarterly, depending on service) payments if you have met the threshold for payment. The threshold is the minimum amount your royalties must be before they cut you a check or do automatic deposit.

Now, let's start with hardcover since there's such a big fascination with hardcovers in esoteric publishing. Hardcovers appeal to practitioners who want sturdy copies of their favorite books. They also appeal to collectors if the hardcover in question is done with high quality bindings. You can't do POD hardcovers and get the high-quality binding you would get with an offset print run.

Limited Edition Hardcover – Offset Print Runs (Short Print Runs)

There are so many offset printing companies out there that I certainly could not list them all. Many of them work with local binderies to bind hardcovers. You often can't do all of this online. You'll have to talk to each company individually about your specific project. Then they can tell you what they need and they can give you a price quote. Infernal Colopatiron cost me about $4000 to print and bind 260 copies. 220 were bound a faux black leather, 30 were bound in burgundy bonded leather, and 10 were hand bound in real black leather with French end papers. That was money I had to pay out of my pocket up front, and money that I eventually made back by selling all the copies. I also lost my spare bedroom for about a year and a half (for storage) and I spent about five hours a week distributing them. Of course, the more copies you buy, the better the price per unit, but you should be realistic about how many people are going to want the book. If you're virtually unknown, limited edition hardcover is likely not the route you want to go. I only did 260 copies of Infernal Colopatiron because realistically – it was a very specialized book geared toward very specific practitioners of magick (Daemonolaters) and a very niche topic (gate opening and theophany). *The more 401 a book ACTUALLY is, the smaller the audience by default.* This is why so many LEH titles are actually 101 dressed up as 401. Beginner books sell more. So do your homework here. Compare several companies, and ask for samples of cover and paper material. Just working out the details of an offset print run can take a few months. Then, once the company receives your files (for printing), your book is put in a queue and between printing and binding, it can take another 1-2 months' production time. Since I use local printing and binding companies, I simply drive over and pick them up when they're done, thus saving myself shipping fees. However, you may not live in a large enough metropolitan area to be able to do this. So, you'll end up paying for freight shipping, too. (P.S. I highly recommend the services of Denver Book Binding. They can even direct you to a printer they work with to have your book printed!)

Leilah Wendell, a veteran esoteric author who has over 27 years' experience working with offset printing, recommends Thomson Shore and offers this advice to authors seeking offset printing services:

I've been dealing with Thomson-Shore for over 27 years. They are great! Old world quality with today's tech touch! There are MANY, MANY others that are good as well, and many that are terrible. Stay away from Bookmasters and their affiliates. If you Google these days, it's really hard to find old school offset book printers, so please DO take my recommendations seriously if you want a quality product.

One option to make the high cost of offset print runs manageable is to take pre-orders from readers. If people pay up front, you use their money to pay your printing, binding, and shipping costs as well as your costs to ship it to them.

I know, I know. It all sounds like a pain in the ass, and I personally thought it was. That's why I placed *Keys of Ocat* with a small press. So they could deal with all of those details and I wouldn't have to. However, I only made about 1/4 on sales of the same number of books, too. It was a tradeoff and if I was going to do it all over again, I would have simply printed *Keys of Ocat* in standard hardcover, paperback, and eBook and probably have sold just as many copies by now, if not more.

Standard Hardcover – Print-on-Demand

There are two options available for the indie author when it comes to POD hardcover. The first is Lulu, which is a free service unless you want distribution. If you want full distribution you must use one of their ISBN's and you must buy one copy of your hardcover as a "proof", just to make sure it's being printed to your standards before it goes out into the world. I just recently tried this service with a few of my books. So far, I can't complain. The hardcovers Lulu produces are your standard cloth bound hardcovers of the variety typically found on the books in Barnes & Noble bargain bins. Their distribution includes Amazon and distribution through Baker & Taylor and Ingram. This means that anyone with your ISBN can walk into their local Barnes & Noble (or any other brick and mortar bookseller) and go, "Hey – I want to order blah, blah, blah" they give the clerk your book's information and the bookstore can order it for that person. It can take up to three months for your book to find its way into everyone's systems, however. This also makes your hardcovers available via the Lulu website and libraries can go in and order your book for their "metaphysical" section. Especially if readers go in and request it. ::wink, wink::

Lulu also does paperbacks, however — your royalty rates will be lower! So, my advice is to use Lulu.com for hardcovers exclusively, and go with Createspace.com for paperback.

To sign up for Lulu, simply visit their website, sign in, and provide a Paypal address so they can send you payment every time you make at least $10 in book royalties. A few of these sites pay you via Paypal. Others will do paper checks or direct deposit. Having a checking account will be handy, even for Paypal as you can have Paypal dump money directly into your checking account.

Lulu is not your only choice for hardcover print-on-demand. Your other choice is Lightening Source's Indie arm called Ingram Spark. However, this is not a FREE option. Not only are you required to purchase a proof before a book goes into distribution, but there is also a setup fee for each title, and if you change your files, there's a fee every time you have to upload a new file. This means mistakes can start adding up and there is an upfront cost to you that you may, or may not recover through sales. My advice – learn on the free sites first, then move to Ingram Spark if you are comfortable with it. Ingram Spark also distributes to both online and brick and mortar booksellers. The upside of Ingram is that you make more in expanded distribution than you do with Lulu, by a few bucks a copy. Which means you can keep your reader's costs lower. I still prefer Lulu though, especially for books that I'm not sure will sell enough to cover setup fees. I would rather spend my money on editing and cover art services.

Paperbacks

Lulu is fantastic if you want to make sure readers can get a paperback immediately through the Lulu storefront. However, if you're willing to wait about a week after your book is finished, and have it up on Amazon first — go with Createspace.com. Createspace is an Amazon company. They do offer online proofing and free distribution (+free ISBNs if you don't have your own). They also offer the best royalty rates out of all the POD services with regard to paperbacks. So yes – these printing/distribution companies do take a cut! However, it's worth it (to me) so I don't have to be my own distributor. That's what you're paying them to do — print and distribute (processing payments, filling orders, and shipping books out). Createspace has a very simple interface that will walk you through the creation of your book. I get automatic payments into my checking from Createspace and have never had an issue with them not paying me or not reporting sales. You create your own prices on each book, btw, and they will tell you how much you get based on the pricing you set. If you need your books to be returnable – you need to use Ingram Spark (practically no royalty, and you get charged for every return) or you need to do offset print runs.

If you use your own ISBNs with Createspace, some distribution methods (like to libraries) will be off limits to you. If you use the free Createspace ISBN – you can get full distribution. Note that when you use others' free ISBNs, they are named as the publisher everywhere and you can't change that. If you want to be able to use your own publishing imprint you need your own ISBNs (one for each edition of the book) and you will have limited distribution. This is not the case with Ingram Spark. You will get complete distribution there with your own ISBNs. They do not give free ISBNs if you don't have your own. Nor can you publish with Ingram Spark without them.

Once your title goes up on Amazon and all the other stores, it will take a few weeks to show up on sites like Barnes & Noble and in catalogs where it can be ordered through brick and mortar stores. That is the pain of publishing — it can be a slow process. Traditional or not.

EBOOKS

Okay, so let's talk about eBooks. The reality is that most esoteric readers want physical copies of books. But sometimes they also want eBooks. EBooks are a sore subject with many esoteric authors because we're often victims of e-piracy as it is. Some might say that putting out eBooks simply helps the book pirates along by making it easier for them to upload copies. After all, DRM (Digital Rights Management) is easy to crack. However, I have learned that esoteric eBooks do tend to sell well and the people who really enjoy your work are going to pay for it. When it comes to eBooks, we shouldn't be so quick to run away from them. I have several eBooks available that are free pdfs on my website. What people pay for is to have it in the format they want it in for their eReader. I actually do sell copies of Modern Demonolatry, for example, on both Kindle and Nook (more so Kindle with esoteric books) even though there is a free PDF of the book on my website and on every occult pirate site on the web. All of my eBooks have also fallen victim to being illegally uploaded. My solution to this? For the longer books, I give more content and graphics in printed versions. The eBooks are bare bones.

There are several ways to go about selling eBooks. The first is to use what we call an aggregate service like Smashwords or Ingram Spark. An aggregate service is one where you format the book to spec and they post your eBook to all the major eBook retailers for you. The alternative is to go to each individual bookseller's online indie publisher site and upload your book directly. I don't use Smashwords for aggregation for my esoteric books, but I do use them for fiction. They also pay via Paypal so you probably ought to set up a Paypal account if you want to use Smashword's services. They have a very detailed "style guide" that your manuscript must follow if you want to be included in the "Premium" catalog. The beauty of it is if you only have to upload one file. The drawback is you make less per eBook because not only do the distributors take a cut to help pay for the server space your book uses, and the upkeep of said servers, but so does Smashwords. That's how they make their service as an aggregation outlet free to you. You can also just sell eBooks on Smashwords without having to have Smashwords distribute to everyone else, which is what I do. You can also choose the formats you will allow readers to purchase.

The three big eBook sellers I encourage every indie to consider is Amazon's Kindle portal called KDP (Kindle Direct Publishing) at kdp.amazon.com. They pay direct deposit or check I believe. Then there's Barnes & Noble's Nook Press at www.nookpress.com (they also pay direct deposit or check). Finally, there is Kobo's Writing Life at www.kobo.com/writinglife/. All of these sites are FREE to authors. I encourage you to sign up for accounts on these websites, and poke around to get yourself familiar with how they work.

Kindle Unlimited is all the rage for a lot of authors nowadays. Basically, when you sign up for Kindle Unlimited, you are giving Amazon exclusive rights to distribute your eBook (i.e. you can't put your eBook on any other site when enrolled in Kindle Unlimited), and your book becomes part of a massive lending library where you are paid for page reads. You won't get rich from page reads, but you still get paid. Usually it's a fraction of a cent per page read.

Let's make a quick checklist of what you'll need when you sign up for these websites:

- Email Address
- Mailing address
- Full name (legal name so they can pay you)
- Social security # (so they can send you your 1099's at the end of the year!) If you are outside the US, I'm not sure what type of tax filing information they'll need.
- Paypal account email address, or bank and checking account information.

Simple - right? Next - let's talk about getting your book ready for publication!

Editing & Formatting

Now that you're all signed up for your printing options, or you have written to the offset printer (or called) to get more information, let's take a look at your completed manuscript. The first step before you publish it is to have it edited.

Yes, I realize you may have run it through a spell checker, but real editing goes beyond that. Let me explain...

Editing

First, most esoteric authors use a lot of words and names not found in your standard spell-check dictionary. It's really easy to use variant spellings of a single name, for example Belphegore, Belphagore, and Belphegor, in a book that spans 250+ pages. The kicker is ALL of those spellings are acceptable, but readers expect consistency because, if they're not too bright (and some aren't), they are going to protest your variant spellings and call them typos, or worse, tell everyone you can't spell and need a good editor. So, you're not just editing for spelling of strange words or names — you're also editing for consistency. If you use Gamigin (Gamagin) in one part of the text but turn around and say Samigina two pages later, the reader who doesn't know they're one in the same just got lost.

Next, a good editing pass checks the book for a logical outline and order, and examines the prose for smooth flow. Also, a good edit should point the author in the direction of areas that could use more explanation (i.e. address unanswered questions), less explanation, and clarification.

A good editing pass will also address any wonky grammar. (Reading your book aloud to yourself, or using MS Word's text to speech feature, helps in this area, too.)

Now here's the thing — writers shouldn't edit their own work past the second or third draft. That isn't to say you can't edit and revise and such, just that by the time you're close to sending your work out into the world, it needs to be seen by someone with a fresh set of eyes. Someone who has a solid grasp of the English language (or whatever language you're writing in). They don't have to be perfect. Hell – humans aren't perfect and I don't care how much you pay for an editor – there will always be that one typo or grammatical error, or even spelling consistency error that gets past even the most anal retentive Grammar Nazi. It is what it is. But this doesn't mean you shouldn't try.

Now let me point out that there are two types of editors:

The first is the content editor. This is the person who can go through your manuscript, ask questions, point out areas that require clarification, point out missing parts, point out excessive explanation, judge everything for flow and logical order, and catch the most obvious grammatical and consistency errors. A good content editor should probably know a little something of the subject you're writing about. Otherwise, they may ask too many questions and not really understand most of what they're reading. Unless you're writing a beginner text, I'd stay away from a content editor who isn't familiar with your subject matter to some degree.

The second editor is your line editor. This is your standard proof reader. Proof readers will go through and check for grammar and spelling mistakes as well as mistakes in consistency. These people have an uncanny attention to detail and may read a bit slower than some of us, but every error will pop out at them.

Now – here's the kicker, if you want a professional editor (or two), it will cost you a pretty penny. Professional editors can go for $500+ per manuscript. Sometimes you can get them for a bit cheaper if they like your work. If you're like a lot of indie writers, you don't have that kind of money to spend. This is where dedicated fans of your work, close friends (who are willing to be HONEST), and even honest family members might come in. Not only will friends and family often work for pizza and beer, but if you mention them in the acknowledgments and give them a free copy, most will be happy to help in any way they can.

Dedicated fans of your work, or fans turned friends, will often jump at a chance to be what we in the business call a "Beta Reader". These are the first people who get a look at a book, and many of them will happily give your book a read (and an editing pass) for the price of a free copy. I often pay beta readers in books. It's win-win for both of us. They get free books and honorable mentions, and I get a fresh set of eyes. If you can't afford a professional editor, I recommend you find one person to serve as a content editor, at least one person proficient in the language to act as a line editor, and at least two beta readers. This gives you four sets of eyes (and your own) to scour the manuscript for errors.

Give these people your manuscript, permission to be brutal, and let them rip it to shreds. Also – give them a deadline so they know when you'll need the manuscript by. If you leave that as an open-ended invitation, you could be waiting a month, or longer in the case of procrastinators. You're likely going to go through a few people until you find the folks who can meet your deadlines and catch the most errors. Not to mention you'll weed out the weak editors and find those who will happily point out errors without worrying about hurting your feelings. Some people are just too nice to edit effectively. Don't use those people next time, just find someone else.

Let's say you've done this. You've now got, hopefully, either lists of where editing is needed, or you have marked up manuscript copies. Sit down and, one at a time, go through each person's edits and make changes as you see fit. Notice how I don't say you should make every change suggested. You may know something your editor didn't, or your editor could be wrong. Maybe you didn't want to handhold the reader through chapter seven like Beta Reader number two wanted. You're the author AND publisher — you're in control. Ultimately, you're the one who makes the final decision on what gets changed and what doesn't.

Once you've made all your changes, run another grammar/spell check in your word processing program. Yes, I know you did it before – but do it again. Sometimes editing leaves extra words in a sentence, or random typos. Not to mention a final pass on your part is likely to catch those errors everyone else missed. Once all the changes are made – save the file anew under a different file name. For example, let's say your file is called Lucifer. You might name it Lucifer Edited. Or Lucifer Final. Once you are sure your manuscript has been sufficiently edited – now it's time to format.

I am going to presume you use MSWord or an equivalent word processing program. If you do not, I apologize. However, I've found over the years that most word processing programs work the same and, just a tip — a lot of these publishing sites work with MS Word and Adobe PDF. Do keep this in mind.

First thing's first. Make sure you used the PAGE BREAK option at each chapter break. I find this makes my life a little easier.

If you're going to do an eBook, too – save your file to a new file and call it [Book Title] Electronic, and set it aside. It will be formatted differently.

Then go into your final edited file and begin formatting it for print.

Formatting for Print

First change the page layout size to the trim size you want your book to be. Most non-fiction books are 6 x 9. That's also the size of your standard hardcover. It's a good size for non-fiction paperbacks, too. For fiction, go with 5.5 x 8.5 or 5 x 8.

Once you've done this you'll notice your page count will adjust itself. Keep your margins at least .5 top and bottom, and .25 right and left. Some use .5 all the way around. You want more space at the top and bottom to accommodate headers and footers. Adjust accordingly. You may want to look at some of the published books in your library and find formats you like and try to emulate them. Don't forget to fully justify your margins! You don't want a ragged right edge in the printed version of your book. You also don't want double-spacing so make sure you change everything back to single space if you're one of those writers trained to double-space everything.

Next, go in and set your headers and footers. Usually publishers will include the title and author name in the header and page numbers in the footer. Sometimes all of this will be in the header. In other books, the author name and name of the book alternate on odd and even page numbers. Consider styling features like putting headers and footers in a legible 10-point font using ALL CAPS, Small Caps, and/or special character spacing to get the look you want.

I can't stress enough here that you should use a legible font! You don't want to give your readers headaches or seizures. I've seen books printed in Old English that were horrific and garish. If you want your book to actually be read — use a legible font. If your book seems too large and you want to keep costs down, feel free to decrease to a 10-point font throughout. I am fond of a 10-12 point Garamond. It's smaller than your standard Times New Roman and it looks nice. Arial is far too large and round for my taste. A standard Times New Roman is always a good standby. If you want to use fancy first letters or chapter heads – go for it. Just be careful because some fonts don't always translate well to printable pdfs.

Next, go in to the main text of the book. Format your chapter headings. I like starting chapters two inches from the top of the page. That's kind of my thing. You may find you like a different look. Experiment with it. Have fun. It's YOUR book. Make sure all your artwork is placed where you want it. Do this from the beginning of the book to the end.

If you just use one file remember that your page numbers should start on the page the book starts on, and this should be an odd page number. I point this out because you must remember that each ODD page number (if the file) is the front of a page, and each EVEN page number will (numbered or not) fall on the back of a page. This formatting trick can take some getting used to in Word and I personally find it rather fickle, which is why I started out using three files. The FRONT PAGES, the CONTENT FILE, and the BACK PAGES. In this case, the odd pages are still the front of the page, and the even numbers are still the back of the page. **Each file should contain an even number of pages.**

If you're creating one file – make sure it, too, has an even number of pages. It just makes things easier.

For front pages: go in and create your title pages, copyright pages, dedication, acknowledgments, and table of contents. Don't forget to add your ISBN to your copyright page. You need one ISBN per edition of the book. That means your ISBN for the paperback is going to be different than the hardcover. Usually eBooks don't require ISBNs unless you are uploading to iTunes. Just remember that if you're doing both a hardcover AND paperback, you need to put the right ISBN (you'll need one number for each) in the interior file before uploading. You might again change the file names to LUCIFER HARDCOVER INTERIOR or LUCIFER PAPERBACK INTERIOR.

At this point you can save your file to PDF (embed the fonts by clicking the option to make it ISO compliant). If you're using an actual project layout program like Page Maker or you're super proficient with Word formatting, this might be the end of your journey for your interior file.

To use just one word file, you would use section breaks, unlink all the headers and footers, and then modify headers and footers for the actual content section of the manuscript. It's actually pretty simple once you learn how to do it.

I used to struggle with Word. We didn't always get along when it came to formatting. For ease of use, I used to create three separate files. FRONT PAGES (title page, copyright page, dedication, acknowledgments, and table of contents) and the BACK PAGES (additional pages at the end of a book that may advertise your other in-print titles, or blank pages to give your MS an even page count divisible by four), and then my actual content file. I did this because I used to do my book formatting in a very specific order. First, I set up the book in Lulu.

I upload my raw Word files directly to Lulu, and Lulu makes me a print-ready interior PDF. I do one for the hardcover and I do one for the paperback. I check both over to make sure they look right. I save the Paperback interior to my hard-drive. This is the file I use to upload to Createspace as the interior file. Easy peasy.

If you're worried about doing this – there are places you can hire to do your formatting for you. It can cost anywhere from $100-$500 per book. Personally, I don't pay for what I can do myself.

Next comes the cover-art, but we'll talk about that in the next chapter.

Formatting EBOOKS

I'll be honest with you. I hate formatting eBooks. If you have graphs, pictures, and tables, formatting an eBook can be a nightmare and you may as well just save up money and pay a professional service to do it for you. I have two books I couldn't format into eBook for the simple fact that I honestly didn't even know where to begin. They're monsters. Createspace finally contacted me and offered to put The Complete Book of Demonolatry in eBook for me (for free) because it was a bestseller.

So first prepare your ELECTRONIC interior file by including your Electronic title page, copyright page (add ISBNs if you want to, some stores require them, others do not), content page, and so on. Basically, all of your "Front Matter". Then go through the book and bold and center your chapter heads.

You don't need page numbers or headers or footers. None of that will show up in an e-reader. You also don't need to worry about fully justified margins since the eReader does its own thing there, too. Actually, for eBooks – minimal formatting is best.

Again, stick with legible fonts. Don't use a font larger than 16 point. Times New Roman is fine here. No double-spacing or typical submission manuscript format.

Add any END PAGE material, like sneak peeks at your next book, or more information about the author or whatever you want to stick back there.

Now save it. If you're using the latest version of word, you now have a *.docx file named something like [Your file name] ELECTRONIC. This file should work for Kindle(Amazon), Nook(B&N), and Kobo. You will upload this file AS IS directly onto all of those publishing platforms. It *should* upload pics and all. On Nook, you will have the option to use the online viewer to check the book out to make sure the formatting isn't screwed up.

It used to be that Kindle only allowed HTML files, especially if you wanted your graphics to show up. I don't know if that's true anymore, but just in case, this method should help you upload books with graphics. Take that same docx file, save it as FILTERED HTML, and call it [Your file name] KINDLE*.html. If you have a lot of photos you'll now have a new file folder on your desktop named after your file. Go to your file manager, copy your html file into that file folder with images. Using a zip program, zip it up and call it FILENAMEKINDLE.zip. This will be the file you upload to Kindle. If your book has no graphics, you can just upload the raw html file directly to the platform. DONE. (As a side note here - Since this was written - Amazon's KDP now allows you to upload Word files and I think the word files look better. Though I don't know if they made graphics easier.)

Finally – for Smashwords — it likes ePubs or old Word docs (not *.docx) for upload. Now, take your word file and save it one more time as a Word 97 *.doc. Upload this one to Smashwords. Now — if you are using Smashwords as an aggregate — you need to follow their formatting guidelines to the letter. One of the big no-noes for eBooks is DO NOT USE TABS or spaces at the beginning of a new paragraph. Instead, set up your word processor to automatically indent the first line of each paragraph.

As you go, you'll refine your method of file creation. Who knows, a few years from now, it may be easier. The industry is changing so quickly, you can't determine if there will be an easier way six months from now. So keep your eyes open!

And that's it! You now have a Hardcover, a Paperback, and eBook. Smashwords and Lulu will both show your books almost immediately. It can take up to 72 hours for both Amazon and B&N to show eBooks, and paperbacks, once submitted for approval can take 24 hours for the proof to be ready, and 72 hours after that to show up on Amazon. A few more weeks to show up in other retailers. But more about that later when we talk about Launching.

Next, we need to talk about Cover Art because you need to have cover art.

Cover Art

Cover art is one of those things that indie writers either hit or miss. If you don't have an artistic bone in your body — hire it out. Seriously.

However, if you're broke or you want to use your own art you are going to need some computer savvy and know-how to make a decent cover. I personally use MS Publisher and GIMP (Free!) for covers I have done myself.

I always start with a cover the SAME trim size as my book. It makes it less likely it will be rejected. Smashwords requires that your cover be at least 1,400 pixels wide with a height greater than width. The other sites all have interesting specifications for their covers, too. Usually if it works for a print site, it will work for all of them. Make sure all cover art is at least 300dpi!

I'm not going to tell you HOW to make a cover because my software skills when it comes to GIMP or PaintShop or PhotoShop are beginner at best and I tend to hire most of my covers out. My cover lady uses MS Publisher anyway. So I can't help you there.

I will, however, re-state what I've learned about designing covers over the years. First – keep about three-quarters of an inch on the edge of the cover free from text. You don't want anything accidentally cut off. That margin will keep you from having your covers rejected from paperback or hardcover printing. Also — use templates! They help.

This is probably redundant to blog posts I've written in the past regarding covers, so here is a recap of my personal tips for creating good cover art (feel free to disagree — art is subjective!) —

1. **Don't use artwork you did yourself if you're not a good artist.** There are sites on the web where you can purchase artwork or photographs that can be used on books. Make use of them if you're not artistic. If you are an artist – be honest with yourself here. Is your work eye-catching? Or could it be turning readers off?

2. **Make sure your cover image is AT LEAST 300dpi and is sized right.** I can't believe all of the pixilated and improperly sized (usually stretched) art I see on people's covers. The easiest way to avoid this is to size your cover art the same as the trim size of your book. So, for example, if you're putting out a 5.5" x 8.5" book, make sure your art is at least 300 dpi (dots per inch) and is sized 5.5" x 8.5".

3. **Make sure people can read your title and YOUR NAME.** A lot of covers I've seen have the author's name tiny, at the bottom of the book. I see this on pro books, too and I think it's just bad design in general. You want the reader to remember YOUR name as well as the name of your book. In other instances of bad cover art – one can barely read the title because it's too small, or the font is so gods-awful (or so common) that it just looks bad. Stay away from fonts that are hard to read, too. Sometimes Garamond trumps a common Brush Script. It looks cleaner and classier. And for gods' sake – NEVER use Algerian or Papyrus!! These are two of the most overused, awful fonts I've seen on indie covers. Bleh!

4. **Study professional covers and emulate the ones you like.** Notice how titles and author names are not falling off the covers or sitting right on the top or bottom edge. It's okay to put your title in the middle or at the bottom. Experiment. Do several covers and then let friends judge which one is best. Take that best one, and tweak it.

5. **Many of us have creative friends who are more than willing to help with cover creation.** Take people up on their offers to help or lend an eye. I have some artistic friends who will work for beer and pizza, or a few hundred bucks instead of five hundred. My husband has a good aesthetic eye, too. Find someone with an aesthetic eye to look at your cover and give you some constructive ideas for improvement. Sometimes it's about moving design elements around until they "click".

6. **Keep it simple.** Sometimes simple is better. The more complex the artwork and the font, the busier a cover gets. The busier it gets, the more likely it will be glossed over by readers. If you have busy artwork, use a simple font. If you have simple artwork, a more decorative, but legible, font can dress it up.

7. **Color — Don't be afraid of it.** Use light font colors for dark backgrounds and dark font colors for light backgrounds. Also, don't be afraid to make one word in a title a different color so it will *pop*. Make sure you use font colors that compliment your cover-art, not compete with it. If you really have no sense of style, design, or taste – get someone who does to help you. You'll be glad you did.

All of the publishing websites require that cover art be uploaded as a *.jpg or PDF, so keep that in mind.

Launching & Marketing

Okay – so now you have an edited, formatted book ready for uploading to all the various websites, or submission to your offset printer. Now all that's left is doing your uploads, checking proofs, and waiting for books to populate to each distribution website.

So – for eBooks, click on the "Add a New Book" option and just follow the instructions. Some things handy to have at the ready:

- The exact title of your book.
- The Description of your book (i.e. the text that tells the potential buyer what the book is about)
- The page count printed (you'll need that for a B&N eBook).
- The ISBN for the eBook (optional) – if you have one. If you don't, no worries. Amazon, B&N, Kobo and Smashwords don't require it. iTunes does.
- The price you want to charge for the eBook

Yeah – you could just wing it, but you want most of these things to be consistent across platforms (like description, price, exact title, and author name) and that's easier to do if you can just copy and paste it from one location into the proper box. Now you just follow the prompts. For Kindle, you'll be uploaded an unfiltered html page or Word file. For Kobo and Nook, you'll be uploading Word files, and for Smashwords you'll be uploading old Word files with the *.doc extension. eBooks usually become live within 48 hours on most distribution sites, except Smashwords where availability (on Smashwords anyway) is instant.

For hardcovers or paperbacks via Lulu – upload your Word files with any appropriate ISBN numbers assigned (personally or through your distribution services) on the copyright page for your hardcover and/or paperback editions (remember that each format must have its own unique ISBN), go through and look at the print ready PDF to make sure it looks good, follow the prompts to upload your cover and insert all your info (listed above), then you can order a proof. This will insure distribution across all outlets. If you're not using Lulu for wide distribution – you can skip the proof ordering and just make it live right then and there. Instantly available book. There you go! If you did get a Lulu ISBN and are using them for distribution and did order a proof — when you get the proof, go through it, then log back in and approve your proof. It can take two weeks up to a month for the book to become available to other distributors.

For Createspace, follow the prompts and upload your interior file (with appropriate ISBN #), upload your cover art, or use the cover creator to upload your cover (easier), and save it all. Createspace has a file validation it has to go through. Your cover and interior file will be checked to make sure it's printable. This process takes about 24 hours. They'll send you an email once it's ready for proofing, or if you need to fix errors. Once you log back in to proof you have two options – you can either proof your interior file online via the free online proofer, or you can order a physical proof to look it over before making it live. Once you approve your proof it can take 24-48 hours for the book to start showing up on Amazon, and 2-6 weeks to begin appearing on the sites of other distributors if you chose expanded distribution options.

A lot of this is simple. Just make sure you have a few hours to spare the first time you do it and follow the prompts.

For those of you working with Amazon, once your book(s) can be found on Amazon – go over to authorcentral.amazon.com and set up your Amazon author page. Just log in, follow the prompts, choose your books, wait 24 hours and there you go! You can go in and tweak your Amazon Author Profile at any time.

Ideally you want to wait to announce your book until it's at least available on Amazon and Barnes & Noble. This can take anywhere from 2-4 days after your initial uploads. If you're smart about it, you will plan your release dates and marketing campaigns accordingly and you can give your book an excellent launch! Perhaps a live event to give away copies using video conferencing software like AnyMeeting, or a free chat room. Facebook event pages are also an author favorite for launch parties.

As an esoteric author, you likely have a twitter account, a Facebook page or profile, and a website. Be sure to use all of these outlets to herald your new releases and engage readers in conversation about your new book(s). Using social networking software like Hootsuite will make monitoring all of your social networks and scheduling posts a breeze. Yes — you can schedule posts in advance if you didn't already know this. A little trick: scheduling a week or even a month's worth of posts in advance will free up your time and keep you from spending too much time social networking. Hanging out where your readers hang out helps, too. Forums, discussion groups, and esoteric gatherings are great places to share information about your books, if sharing isn't looked down on.

The biggest rule is DON'T SPAM. That isn't to say don't tweet your book, or post the link in certain places. Just make sure that's not all you're posting. If all you do is advertise, people might pull you out of their news feeds or simply ignore anything you have to say. Some groups will kick you out for just advertising. Show readers that you're a real person with real interests (other than hocking your books) and give them a reason to follow you. Being interesting with something to contribute will sell your books far faster than talking about your books all the time.

Vista Print and many other printing companies like UPrinting offer low cost marketing material for even small print runs for post cards, business cards, and so on. Don't forget local print shops. I wouldn't go overboard with marketing material. Start with 100 bookmarks IF you're going to conventions, doing book signings, or presenting seminars, workshops, or classes. Otherwise they won't do you any good.

If you're printing your own books, like limited edition hardcovers, the industry seems to be going the way of nice presentation for mailing beyond simple bubble or book mailers. I've received limited edition hardcovers wrapped in bio-degradable plastic bags with the publisher's logo on it and embossed stickers holding the bag closed. All of them seem to come with publisher logo bookmarks, or bookmarks with Satanic quotes or whatnot on them. Some have been wrapped in velvet bags and nestled in advertising boxes with the publisher logo on it. Be creative with this. It will make readers remember your book(s) or "Brand".

Remember that for marketing – it's all about branding yourself.

Self-Presentation

Presenting yourself in the best possible light is very important for any author of spiritually driven books. If you have a lot of personal hang-ups, personal vendettas, or life drama — now is the time to start keeping it to yourself or getting rid of it.

People who buy esoteric texts want the authors giving them advice to have their shit together. This means that if you're writing a book about money magick, you shouldn't constantly be bitching about how poor you are. Or if you have a rivalry with a fellow practitioner, you're not constantly libeling or slandering that individual on your social media or in your writing. You need to develop a live and let live philosophy, and if another practitioner's methods annoy you or you don't agree with them - find a way to say it in a way where you aren't naming names or making personal attacks. Attack the process or idea with well thought arguments. Otherwise you're just being petty. Esoteric practitioners turned writers aren't loved for their pettiness. They're loved for the usefulness of the material they're putting out there. You're basically sharing ideas and techniques meant to help other people and inspire them in their own practice. So be mindful of this and behave accordingly.

Authors who make readers feel welcome, and positive, sell more books.

What would you think if your favorite esoteric author consistently posted nude photos of him/herself online? Or sent uninvited dick pics to people they were interested in? What if they constantly complained about their relationships or consistently whined about other practitioners? Wouldn't you be put off? Always ask yourself, "If my favorite esoteric author posted something like this, would I be put off?" If the answer is yes, delete the post or don't post it to begin with.

Another thing readers appreciate in an esoteric author is consistency. Is the author changing religions every other week? Or have they been consistent enough to actually know what they're talking about? It takes a lot of time to learn enough about a subject to be able to write about it effectively. If a practitioner is jumping from religion to religion, or paradigm to paradigm, have they actually learned enough to really know the subject well? These are question you should ask yourself and be honest with yourself about. If you've only been practicing for five years, mostly on the weekends, are you really qualified to write an advanced book about the topic? Readers will be judging you.

Include others in your conversations. Ask readers how they feel about something. Ask them to share their favorite incense recipe, or spell. What is their favorite Asana or breathing exercise? The more you include your readers in the conversation, the more likely they are to buy your books. Remember - we write for readers.

When you are genuinely wrong about something or you've say, or do a thing you shouldn't have - correct yourself or apologize and be genuine about it. Of course, if you were right, or you did nothing wrong - save your apologies.

Do not challenge the reviewers. They are allowed to hate your book. Did someone give your book a bad review? Ignore it and move on. Every author has their critics and every book, even a good book, gets bad reviews. It is what it is. Not everyone will like what you write and that's okay. So, don't confront your reviewers/critics.

If for some reason your reviewers or critics come into your domain and start spouting their venom, you have two choices. 1. You can delete, block, and ignore. Or 2. You can engage them with a level head, a sound argument, and no name calling. Be the bigger person if you can. If you can't, it's always better to go with number one.

Dear Aspiring Occult Author

Dear Aspiring Occult Author,

Thank you for writing to me. You're the fifth aspiring occult author I've heard from this week. There certainly are a lot of you. Let me answer your questions in the same order in which you asked them.

1. You want to know which of my Daemonolatry titles makes me the most money and I totally understand that it's a research question. But let me be clear for a moment — the money should be the LAST thing you are concerned with. One doesn't write esoteric books for money. It's a labor of love. I can't believe how many aspiring esoteric authors I meet who really believe they can make $1,000+ every month right out the gate writing occult books. I never got into writing books about Daemonolatry for the money. If that were the case – I would have quit long ago and we'll get to why in a minute. I write the books I write because I believe in the work I'm doing and I want to

share that work with like-minded people who might find it inspiring to their own practice.

Do some of my books make money? Yes, but not as much money as you think. Remember that authors of paperbacks and eBooks, and sometimes even hardcovers (depending on the publisher, or distribution outlet) literally make their living $1-2 at a time. That means in order to make $1,000 you need to sell 500-1000 books a month, and the average occult title (especially niche titles) is lucky to sell 10-85 copies a month. Even less if you're unknown in the occult world or have no publisher support. So, at $1-$2 apiece, how much is that? Don't forget to factor in that after the first month, sales often start to wane. You must constantly be able to produce new material (good material that readers will find beneficial) to create a continuous income. This means you must be prolific. If it takes you one year to write a book... well...you do the math. You're not going to get rich writing occult books.

My advice? Instead of trying to find which topic you can cash in on, why not focus on writing about the topics you love and have the most experience with? Stop worrying about what everyone else is doing and do what you love.

I think it's great that after a 2-5 years of practicing magick you feel inspired to write about it. Of course, I had already been practicing for fifteen years before I wrote Modern Demonolatry (and it wasn't very good – it was smacking of a first book). It took me another seven years before I felt confident enough to write The Complete Book of Demonolatry and another five years after that before I felt I had written a REALLY GOOD book (Infernal Colopatiron) about Daemonolatry. Keys of Ocat was another book I was extremely proud of. All my years practicing and experiencing the Daemonic went a long way to making my books what they are. Experience does seem to count for something when it comes to readers in this genre. So, get the experience before writing the book!! You'll be happy you did.

2. I am so happy to hear you are writing your memoirs. I think writing about our lives can be a cathartic exercise, but no, as a publisher, I can't publish your memoirs and I don't recommend you self-publish them either. Sorry. You're only twenty-three years old. Published memoirs are only interesting if you've done something really inspiring or lived a full and interesting life. So far, based on what you've told me, you've just now moved out of your parents' house, haven't been outside the state you live in, and haven't even gotten your life started yet. By the time you reach a point in your life where your memoirs might be worthy of publication, I'll be long retired or dead. Best to save finding a publisher, or considering self-publishing, until you're in your fifties or sixties.

3. I also think it's awesome that you also want to try your hand at fiction in addition to writing occult books! I'm so glad I could inspire you and make it look easy. You know, I was a fiction author long before I started penning books about Daemonolatry. I even

went to college for writing and publishing because I've wanted to be a novelist since I was in grade-school. I have to admit, I do find it a bit concerning that you don't have a Goodreads page, and that the last novel you said you read was The Great Gatsby, something everyone read in High School English. Oh yes, I forgot, you read Stephen King's Pet Sematary, too. You also seem to be struggling for titles when I asked you what the last five novels you read were. Or I can tell you're just puking out titles of popular fiction because you can't actually remember what the last novel you read was. I am genuinely interested in what you're reading because writers are readers and it's my opinion that those who don't read fiction (voraciously), really have no business writing it. Mostly because if you don't read and you haven't practiced craft, then you likely don't know how to craft a story. That comes with time, work, and a lot of reading and writing. I have never met a "natural" storyteller. So no, as a publisher I will not consider your book of short fiction or your first novel until I can be relatively certain you've actually read some fiction in the genre you wish to write in. Self-publish if you must, but don't expect it to do well. This leads me to my next answer.

4. No. I can't consider your idea for a book or novel or story for publication. I'm still an editor/publisher and if you want me to consider publishing your work, you need to send me a completed manuscript. Everyone has ideas for books, novels, and stories. Everyone. It's whether they can get it out onto the page that matters. Can you write a book independently from beginning to end without being

hand-held by an editor? That's what real writers do. You can tell me all day long that you're a writer, but until I see something you've completed on your own, something more than just an essay or poem, you're just an *aspiring* writer.

5. You asked my advice regarding your idea to quit your day job, declare yourself a writer, and jump into the fray. I realize that at twenty-three you would prefer to write instead of getting a regular job because writing is easier (::snort::) and doesn't require you to have to wake up before noon, but really – please listen to my advice here — you need food, shelter, and clothing. Please don't quit your day job yet. It took me 20 years of writing professionally in my free time (in addition to working 50+ hours a week) to finally start making a living from my writing. And by "a living" I mean making a better yearly salary than I made at my accounting job. And guess what? I still keep a part-time day job. Why? Because having health insurance, and a reliable income for my reliable bills is important to me. Plus, most publishers pay quarterly. If you self-publish, you get paid once a month. That means you're only getting paid once a month or every three months. It's NOT like a regular job where you get paid 2-4 times a month. This means that you must be better at budgeting your money. I'm really not trying to discourage you from trying out writing as a career, I'm just trying to keep you from having to move back in with your parents or save you from living under a bridge. I want to provide honest encouragement. I'm not one to blow sunshine up your ass. If that's what

you're looking for, you might try seeking a different writer for career advice.

6. Thank you for sharing your rather interesting story about your family involvement in the occult. I often get this same story from a lot of the would-be occult writers who contact me. So I know a lot of generational people. Some legitimate, some I question. Either way let's face it – you can be generational and still be a noob and/or a not-so-good writer, and I will be able to tell what's what. You can't tell me, for example, that your family practiced Khemetic Daemonolatry and that your family matron is Hecate or Ashtaroth. That doesn't really make sense and I will raise an eyebrow at that unless there's a good explanation as to how that happened. So, if you're going to spin me a story, please at least tell me a good one or just drop the pretense and tell me you wrote a book about Daemonolatry. Because a generational influence (or not) doesn't make publishers want to publish your book. A well-written book with interesting, fresh and new ideas is what makes them want to publish a book. Give us something we've never seen in print before and make it interesting. I'm interested even if you made it up, worked with it, and got results. I'm not opposed to "Unverified Personal Gnosis". I enjoy reading about other people's creative implementation of magickal techniques. If you're self-publishing, don't expect readers to be impressed with alleged generational connections either. Some get downright pissed-off at authors who say they're generational. Depends on the reader.

7. I hear at least once a month from an aspiring writer that they are concerned about being viewed as competition by already established writers. Competition? That doesn't really make sense in the writing world because readers interested in any topic will likely read a variety of writers on said topic and continue reading those writers they liked best. With fiction, who readers like will vary from reader to reader. Oftentimes, writers share readers (regardless genre). Sure – you want to attract the most readers you possibly can, but you don't do it by trying to take other writers off the playing field, or by trying to turn readers against other writers. You attract and earn readers by writing the best books you possibly can. So really, the only person you compete with is yourself and your last book.

You ally with other authors and SUPPORT EACH OTHER because your readers become their readers and vice versa when you team up like that. They scratch your back if you scratch theirs. See what I'm saying?

Besides – most of the folks who contact me haven't written anything publishable yet (or haven't even written anything), so why they would think they're competition is beyond me. You can't be competition if you aren't even on the field playing the game yet. But that said – if you think writing is about competing with other writers about who's better, you've kind of missed the point. Jealousy in this line of work may exist, but those who behave like jealous brats rarely make it to the top.

8. This essay you've written is, at most, a chapbook or pamphlet. It's not a book. No, I will not put it in limited edition hardcover (nor should you), or give you 3/4 the book's cover price. Reality check time – you're not Stephen King. You're an unknown author with a chapbook, currently indistinguishable from the hundreds of other authors with chapbooks out there. Sorry, but until you have a big following, have put out full length books, and have some impressive sales numbers, a publisher can't justify higher royalties or limited edition hardcovers. If you want that, self-publish.

Now I'd like to offer some advice based on our correspondence since you wrote me asking for advice.

Whether you realize it or not, convincing others you can write does extend to your correspondence with them. I am concerned you are not familiar with proper punctuation or sentence structure. Also, text-speak is highly inappropriate when you are corresponding with publishers. It makes you look like someone who isn't serious about a writing career. I have rejected good books, idea-wise, because in order to make them publishable they would need to be completely rewritten by someone with a command of the language. So really, some people just aren't writers and never will be unless they commit themselves to learning how to write well. If your manuscript needs that much clean up, forget it. If you are committed though, hire an editor.

You mentioned having an interest in publishing your own work. I wrote an entire series of web articles about self-publishing esoteric works. Please read it because it will tell you a lot of what you need to know. If you can't make it past the second or third article, forget it — stick with traditional publishing (i.e. getting a publisher to do all that for you).

I have also written an article about what new authors can expect with their first small press publishing contract.

Overall I want to tell you to keep writing because if this truly is your calling – you can succeed! Where there's a will, there's a way.

Good luck with your writing career!

Sincerely, Steph.

**This letter is to no one in particular. Its audience is a composite drafted from the numerous aspiring occult authors who contact me every month asking for advice about their careers, ideas, and books. Each point in this letter represents the most common questions and scenarios I encounter when corresponding with young, aspiring occult authors.

***For context, please remember that I'm both a writer and the acquisitions editor for DB Publishing. I work on both sides of the publishing fence. Hence the reason I get people asking if I'll publish their work.

Should Knowledge Be Free?

Several times this past week I was chastised for writing occult books for money. Well, not directly, but indirectly. Let's just say the topic came up several times. I really think this is something that needs to be addressed because I think this attitude of "knowledge should be free" is part of a larger problem — that problem being e-Piracy.

It seems in the occult world, pirates use the "you should give it away for free because knowledge should be free" as an excuse to pirate books about magick and spirituality.

So first let me give you some background and the TRUTH about why I started writing esoteric books and why I still write them and ultimately why I, as an author, should get paid even though some folks think knowledge should be free.

My first esoteric text, Modern Demonolatry was published back in 1999. I wrote the book after friends requested I write an introductory, pre-initiate text for those starting out in Demonolatry. The reason my friends requested I write the book is because I had, three years prior, gotten a B.A. in English with a creative writing emphasis and I was one of the priestesses of TSL. I was also, at the time, an aspiring novelist.

The truth is I've been a writer even longer than I've been an occultist (by about 4-5 years). I never went into writing thinking I would write about the occult and I never went into the occult thinking I would get into writing about the occult. These were two separate interests that happened to overlap when an opportunity fell into my lap. I agreed to write the book because I believed in the project and because my mentor/teacher and my friends asked me to. I wrote the book for them and fellow Demonolaters and I wrote it for the sake of education. We needed a pre-initiate text and I was the only person in the group who everyone agreed could write the book. And so I did.

Sadly, back then, there were NO books about the subject anywhere and all we had were pamphlets that volunteers typed up one at a time. After a lot of the major publishers turned down the project, and told me it really wasn't a book they wanted to publish (because it was too controversial and too niche), a friend of mine who owned a small publishing company went ahead and published 100 copies of the book for us. We figured it was just as well and decided we should probably just keep our texts within our small community anyway. It turned out those copies went very quickly and the book sold-out within months.

Not to mention more than half the books were sold to the public. In all fairness let me say right now that Modern Demonolatry was not my best work and it was very amateurish. But then it wasn't meant as a mass-produced volume or as something that was ever supposed to be seen outside our small community.

We wanted to do more books, but back then publishing wasn't an easy endeavor and it was expensive. Not to mention printers were wary of printing such stuff, and my friend in the small press had temporarily closed shop due to a money flow issue. In that time, our groups kind of kept to ourselves so we went back to our typed pamphlets.

Meanwhile, I was getting phone calls at my residence from people who had tracked me down looking for copies of Modern Demonolatry. I even had publishers coming out of the woodwork making me offers on the book. I could have very easily SOLD OUT and given Demonolatry to the mainstream, and trust me – I had cash offers. But I didn't. Evidently that small, amateur book had made a huge impact. Clearly there was a need for these kinds of books. But we still didn't have the backing we needed to re-publish the book.

I kept getting calls until, in 2005, a friend sent me a link to Lulu Press. That's when print-on-demand publishing technology became a do-it-yourself deal. It eliminated the up-front costs for me, and gave me a way to put Modern Demonolatry back into print for all the people who had been bugging me for copies. My groups also convinced me to print the companion study guide, Lessons in Demonolatry. It was at this point we decided to formally create DB Publishing which was a publishing company by Demonolaters for Demonolaters. We were going to use it to print books just for people in our small community. Little did we know that our books would be valued by other practicing magicians and Satanists, as well as solitary Demonolaters world-wide. We were filling a niche and every title we put out has always been with the end goal to provide reference material to practicing Demonolaters and Demonolatry magicians. Not for money. In those early days, I would have written some of those older books for my close group of friends whether anyone outside our community wanted them or not. That's the reality of it. (But times have changed, I now have limited time and mouths to feed.)

So that's how I fell into writing esoteric books and how DB Publishing got started.

Now, I do realize that nowadays everyone in the LHP has written a book and followed our lead and printed their own. I get it. I also know of A LOT of authors who write to capitalize on the occult community and they do a bang-up job. I can legitimately understand people pirating copies of out-of-print books as well. I also understand the economics of limited edition hardcovers. So, I can see why some people may be disgusted by those in the occult world who write books just to make a buck. I understand. I've read some of the "darkest most sinister books of [insert Daemon name here]" and they were all complete bullshit. Hell, I even collect the limited-edition hardcovers myself. Some of the books are good – some suck ass. It really depends on the author and if they're trying to baffle you with bullshit and make a buck, or if they're genuine. Trust me – you can tell. Just read a preview – and if they don't offer a preview — run.

I know there will be some who don't believe me, but admittedly I have never really looked at a book and made my decision on whether to write it based on the kind of money I thought it would make. For the most part I print paperbacks because they're affordable and accessible. The only reason we did Infernal Colopatiron in limited edition hardcover was A. To discourage dabblers, B. Offer up something to the collectors who were requesting advanced level, heirloom quality books for permanent libraries (yeah – I get requests for that ALL THE TIME), and C. Give serious Demonolatry magicians books just for them that aren't cheap throw away paperbacks. But again — I wrote the book for the Demonolatry community and the generational set — not the curious, dabblers, or the casual weekend magician.

Truth be known, most of our Demonolatry books have sold less than 200 copies. We really are a small niche publisher. I write books I am passionate about, and that I believe will be the most beneficial to the community at any given time. I also listen to my readers and give them what they want. But because publishing takes TIME and MONEY – I HAVE TO GET PAID and so do our editors, artists, and other production staff. Otherwise I can't afford to do it.

Now I admit that I make enough money with DB Publishing to keep the publishing house open, and to pay my electric bill and part of my grocery bill every month. [A little more now in 2016.] So, while I'm NOT making money hand over fist (and I never expect to), I am making enough from writing the books for it to make a difference to my income and to be able to offer editors and artists compensation for the work they do for us, whether it be cash or free copies.

I also write fiction and I also have a part-time day job. The part-time day job (about 32 hours a week) is for a small reliable income for my always reliable bills, and the rest of my income is made from writing fiction. So technically I have two jobs and I work about 80 hours a week total.

This means that YES – I do count on book sales as a part of my income.

Now before you scream, "How dare you!" let me tell you what the life of a real professional writer is really like. I'm not sitting here eating bon-bons and taking huge vacations. I don't have butlers or maids or drive a Mercedes. I am the sole provider for my family (two adults, three cats). I do have a personal assistant who helps with email and social media, but I can only afford him for six hours a month ($60). I can't even begin to tell you how many times I've had people tell me they thought I was making six figures as an author. For me, six figure years are rare, and usually correspond with a bestseller in fiction. Other writers' results may vary.

First – writing is not a hobby for me, or for any professional writer. I passed the stage of hobby writing when I started having to hire an accountant and itemize my deductions on my taxes because of my writing income. Professional means you make a real, living taxable wage from doing something. While the bulk of that living wage is from writing fiction, some of it is from writing esoteric books.

If that offends anyone – I'm sorry.

Since the IRS doesn't think my writing is a hobby and considers me a professional writer it means I should treat my writing as such, too. Mind you the esoteric books will ALWAYS be a labor of love for me and when I run out of interesting things to write about – I will stop writing about magick and Demonolatry because I refuse to write about anything I'm not passionate about. I considered quitting the Demonolatry writing gig this and passing the torch to someone younger than me. It was my mentor and a larger part of the Demonolatry community that convinced me to stay on.

Second – let me tell you what real professional writers do for a living because I think there's some confusion about that.

I wake up at 6:30 or 7am. I make some coffee and maybe grab some breakfast. I take a quick shower. By the time 7:30-7:45 rolls around I am in front of my computer. I go through my e-mail, answer it, contact editors, printers, readers, and so on as needed. By 9am I'm writing. I write from 9am to noon, usually with a break here or there to get up and stretch my legs. I stop for lunch. Then I sit down and write from about 1pm to 5 or 5:30 with a break here or there to get up and stretch my legs. Sometimes I'll use the break to get on the Fit Desk, get some exercise (to ward off deep vein thrombosis, a job hazard), and read publishing news. Some days I have to gather and sort receipts, look at sales reports, and work on marketing. Other days I edit, research, or toss cover art back and forth between the artists and me. I'm always social networking not because I'm narcissistic, but because I'm marketing my books or interacting with readers and fellow practitioners.

Point being that writing is a REAL job. I spend well over 40 hours a week at the writing gig.

An acquaintance who told me she has mixed feelings about esoteric authors who make money from their books also told me mere hours later that she wouldn't work for less than $10 an hour.

Let me break this down for everyone: I generally sell between 50-70 books a day (about 1/4 or less being esoteric) and make anywhere from .35 cents to $2 a copy per book. Most of my books generate under $2 a copy (don't forget that I have to pay distributors, editors, artists, production people). I'm just the author and that's my cut after it's all said and done. I average anywhere from $60 -$90 a day and the IRS takes 40% of that. What can I say? Self-employment taxes are higher than a regular job. Now, if I work 8 hours a day for five days a week writing, which is 40 hours a week (usually it's more because I often work weekends, too), that means I make roughly $10 an hour as a writer. If I sell less than that then I make less than that per hour.

She wouldn't work for less than $10 an hour – but she expects I should???

I found that very amusing. After all – I'm working almost 80 hours a week to everyone else's 40, and yet somehow, I'm not even allowed to make the scant $10 an hour writing that I make, without offending the same people who would not work for less than $10 an hour.

And this is how ePiracy of occult books is justified by some people. They really believe writers are making money hand over fist, and that a writer should not be allowed to make any portion of their living, no matter how small, on esoteric work. Somehow these people think it's wrong. Probably because they don't realize that writing is a REAL JOB that requires REAL HOURS and REAL WORK.

Not to mention the cost of printing and binding books isn't cheap, folks. Part of the cost of a paperback or hardcover is in the production. Part of the cost of eBooks is keeping the file on a file retrieval system and paying someone to maintain that system. Not to mention there are A LOT of people (not just authors) involved in producing a book. This includes editors, layout and cover designers, printers, binders, distributors, IT professionals, and marketers. Really, when you think knowledge should be free – think of all the people who spent hours and hours (away from their loved ones who they have to provide for) working on that book to make that knowledge easily available to you.

Is their work and time worth nothing?

Would you work for free?

If you wouldn't work for less than $10 an hour – why should those who provide you with knowledge work for less than $10 an hour?

Do you think your college professors or children's school teachers should work for free? No? Then why esoteric writers?

Yes – I get that there are some douches out there who really are just trying to make a buck (those channeling Daemons and writing the darkest of dark sinister books), but what about those of us who really do write to educate or share information? Aren't we allowed to at least make a living wage?

Nothing in life is free. As an acquiring editor over at Llewellyn pointed out – everything in life is about the exchange of energy. You give your boss your time, body, and mind for so many hours a week in return for a paycheck that you, in turn, use to obtain goods and services in order to live. Authors – even esoteric authors (and everyone who works the publishing industry) works to make the knowledge accessible to you, in an easy to follow organized format, in exchange for money (i.e. energy) that we can then use to buy goods and services in order to live.

I see nothing wrong with this.

It may not be an ideal situation or an ideal world, and if I could live on nothing but air and love for writing and sharing my knowledge – I would happily give away everything I write for free. But that's not how the world works and a girl does have to eat, and so does her family who depends on her income. Those are the cold, hard facts of life. I give my readers plenty of free reading material in my blog posts, and in the few books that I freely give away on demonolatry.org.

But for the most part I charge for my writing and I am not sorry for it. Knowledge isn't free. It takes a lot of energy to produce educational materials, which is essentially what esoteric authors do. I am also sharing my knowledge, experience and research and years of hard work (I didn't come by my knowledge via osmosis). I, for one, think that's worth at least $10 an hour, if not more.

The Future of Esoteric Publishing

Recently I've been reading a lot of blogs with posts about the future of esoteric publishing. Some people have a great deal of optimism – others don't.

Admittedly, as both a reader AND writer of esoteric books – I'm finding myself in the naysayer camp. I'm not optimistic at all. Mostly because so much crap is being churned out of the limited edition hardcover market. I won't name any names because that's tacky. But I will say that when it comes to limited edition hardcovers – it's hit or miss on what's good and what isn't. Sadly, the market is chock full of 101 nonsense being passed off as 401 in hundreds of pages of waxing philosophic prose that is great for mental masturbation, but not much else. I'm an actual practicing magician — not an armchair theorist. I don't give two fucks about so-and-so's thoughts on the nature of deity. Good for him/her. My experience is likely different.

I'm also an actual "trained" writer. I have a degree in English (Creative Writing) with a minor in Journalism folks. I had a 4.0 GPA in my major. No, having a degree doesn't mean I write 100% perfect prose all of the time, but it does mean I know a thing or two about writing.

In college, there was a professor who always told us: "If you cannot make a difficult subject understandable in as few words as possible – you do not understand your subject matter enough to be writing about it."

I agree. If you look at the plethora of nonsense being printed, you'll see exactly what I mean. Perhaps if some of these authors would put away the thesaurus and give up the extended metaphors and run-ons, we could let the real writers write real books that help real working magicians.

If you want to sit in your armchair debating the nature of deity, or spend your time walking readers through your personal take on the Tree of Life or the Qliphoth, great, but do it in fewer words, okay? As a student of the esoteric and as a working magician, I know that I'd rather be in the temple or lab doing actual rituals, magick, and experiments that ultimately lend far more practical insight into such matters.

Maybe it's just me and others like me.

Let me be up front with how I feel if I haven't been already — MOST of the books the occult publishing market is churning out these days are not conducive to the advanced practitioner. The books cater to beginners, dabblers, "image" magicians who only want the darkest, most evil, and scariest books, and people too afraid to "do it wrong". Yes, I acknowledge there are a few readers out there who love the "philosophy" books, but I assure you, none of these writers compare to Socrates. If you want some wonderful spiritual fodder to chew on – try the Ancient Greek philosophers. I guarantee you they can say the same things in fewer words, and without the circular metaphor. If anyone knew Daimons – the Greeks most certainly did.

Of course, catering to the dabblers, beginners, image magicians, and fearful is good for the book business. Yes, I know that's a harsh thing to point out. But think about it – all the crap being printed keeps our current generation of magi, all but the most creative of them, insecure and seeking assistance, thus buying more and more books that all say the same thing, in hopes of figuring out some great "secret". The magick "pill" that cures all ills so-to-speak.

We're being fed crap loads of philosophy being passed off as 'the-one-true-way' and 'the only way to think!' Or the authors tell their readers why all the other authors are just poseurs or fluffy bunnies (i.e. white light new-agers). It's great that the authors want to discourage the "competition", and to share their personal philosophy built on years of their own WORK (hopefully). However – shouldn't we, as authors AND students ourselves, give our readers more? Like *ideas* for *work they can do* to come to their own philosophy about the nature of deity?

Authors OWE their readers more than just a dry, boring diatribe, and a quick mental wank. If you don't know how to write – don't. You're ruining it for hundreds of readers/practitioners and for the *real writers* who don't talk in circular metaphoric bullshit.

If you're an author and you want to write devotional books of meditation, poetry, and art - do it - but don't try to sell it as a 401 grimoire because that's not what it is. Sell it as a devotional. I have no doubt you'll still sell just as many copies. People like poetry and art, and they like to meditate. Imagine that!

Maybe it's just me, but anymore I only buy books about rare, unique, or specific subjects that interest me. There are few authors I'll routinely pick up. I have standards. You should, too.

As a writer, I want to tell readers that it's OKAY to have standards. Just because they say it's bound it goat scrotum or signed in babies' blood doesn't mean you should buy it. Seriously – CONTENT, CONTENT, CONTENT. Fuck the binding unless it's a GOOD book that inspires you. Then go ahead and buy the one bound in the skin of a sacrificed goat with the hidden ciphers in the manuscript.

Buy what you like. Buy what INSPIRES your own WORK. For example: If you hate my books, don't buy them! But if you love them, go for it. If you love the waxing philosophic crap – I guess it's your dime. Enjoy. I just know that a lot of readers are getting tired of it, myself included.

As to the future of occult publishing... I guess it remains to be seen. Hopefully once people realize that writing occult books isn't the "get-rich-quick scheme" some seem to think it is, the drivel will fall to the wayside and the useful books will remain.

Also — Excerpts. Read them! If one isn't provided, don't buy. Any lack of an excerpt is suspect, or should be.

More from DB Publishing & Official Melissa Press

By S. Connolly

- The Complete Book of Demonolatry

- The Daemonolater's Guide to Daemonic Magick

- The Art of Creative Magick

- Daemonolatry Goetia

- Infernal Colopatiron or Abyssal Angels: Redux

- Curses, Hexes & Crossings: A Magician's Guide to Execration Magick

- Honoring Death: The Arte of Daemonolatry Necromancy

- Necromantic Sacraments

- Kasdeya Rite of Ba'al: Blood Rite of the Fifth Satan

- Nuctemeron Gates

- Abyssal Communion & Rite of Imbibement

- Keys of Ocat

- Drawing Down Belial

- Bound By Blood: Musings of a Daemonolatress

- Wortcunning for Daemonolatry – S. Connolly

By M. Delaney

- Sanctus Quattuordecim: Daemonolatry Sigil Magick

By E. Purswell

- Goetic Demonolatry

By Martin McGreggor

- Paths to Satan

Various Authors (Compilation Books)

- My Name is Legion: For We Are Many

- Demonolatry Rites

- Ater Votum: Daemonolatry Prayer

- Satanic Clergy Manual

Forthcoming from DB Publishing & Official Melissa:

- Grimorium Daemonolatrie – S. Connolly & M. Delaney (Melissa)

- Sacrae Infernales – S. Connolly

Workbooks and Journals by S. Connolly

- The Goetia Workbook

- 30 Days of Spirit Work

- The Spirit Workbook

- The Meditation Journal

- Ritus Record Libri

Daemonolater's Guides:

- Daemonic Offerings
- Daemonic Pacts
- Daemonolatry Groups
- Sex, Money, & Power
- Spirit Keeping & Spirit Vessels
- Daemonic Possession
- Daemonic Prayer & Prayer Cords

33089517R00046